Let's redefine
SUCCESS

Written and designed by

María Victoria Alger Velásquez

@victoriaalger_

This book belongs to

____

Have you ever felt you are not enough?

Have you felt lost in the daily routine?

Would you like to see yourself as a loved
and valuable being?

Have you felt overwhelmed with so much information about what is the right thing to do to be successful?

Maybe it is time to think about our own definition of being successful.

This book intends to discover what motivates you and that you find your own path in life.

Let's redefine success...

We all talk and hear about
Success
But,

❶ What is success?

❷ How does a successful person look like?

❸ Is it being successful common for all or
it depends on personal values, culture,
family and environment?

Let's define

Success

1 The accomplishment of an aim or purpose.

2 The fact of achieving something good that you have been trying to do.

3 Something that has a good result or that is very popular.

Let's explore some quotes...

Success is a journey, not a destination.

Arthur Ashe

We have been taught success is about reaching a goal and we forget about the journey. We become rat racers jumping from one goal to another. When we reach that goal usually joy lasts only a short time and we have forgotten to embrace the journey and experience all kinds of emotions through it.

Success is walking from failure to failure with no loss of enthusiasm.

Winston Churchill

It is important to keep our goal in mind because failure will come for those pursuing their dream.

Failure is part of the process.

We must learn from mistakes.

Remember the most valuable lessons come from tough moments.

Enthusiasm is key to recover and continue.

I never dreamed about success, I worked for it.

Estée Lauder

Hard work pays off.

Rome wasn't built in a day.

In a world full of "miraculous results" and fake promises it is easy to forget that the most important things require **a daily dose of attention, sacrifice and love.**

The only place success comes before work is in the dictionary.

Vince Lombardi

How hard is it to understand this.

How valuable is it to accept this.

Are you ready?

Success usually comes to those who are too busy to be looking for it.

Henry David Thoreau

Let's get busy.

There's so much to do.

Use your talents wisely and **shine bright.**

Above all, being successful means that our actions are consistent with our values.

There's a difference between the things you value and your actual values.

Understanding your values helps you to live an authentic and happy life.

Real failure is failing to live by your values, and real success is taking action every day to stand for them.

YOU HAVE TO

WALK THE TALK

PUT YOUR WORDS INTO ACTIONS

Values are attributes of the person you want to be.

personal core values

1. Altruism
2. Appreciation
3. Attentiveness
4. Compassion
5. Courage
6. Determination
7. Empathy
8. Equanimity
9. Generosity
10. Honesty
11. Humility
12. Integrity
13. Kindness
14. Loyalty
15. Self-Reliance
16. Selflessness
17. Spirituality
18. Tolerance
19. Toughness
20. Trustworthiness

GO FOR IT

What does success mean to you? Highlight the actions that best suit you.

1. To maintain and nurture healthy relationships
2. Traveling to different countries
3. Learning new languages
4. Exercising periodically
5. Owning a property
6. Helping others
7. Being there for the ones that need me
8. Learn to listen
9. Own a business
10. Finish my career
11. Having money
12. Meet with family and friends
13. Being famous
14. Being independent
15. Owning a car
16. Having peace of mind
17. Pay debts
18. To live in a beautiful place
19. Sharing important moments with family and friends

20. ____

21. ____

22. ____

23. ____

24. ____

Remember:

- **Each one of us is different.**

- **Being different allows us to complement each other.**

- **We need one another to grow, learn and be successful.**

Write your success story...

Take your time, think of how you picture yourself and the road ahead. Describe how you look, what do you do, who you relate to.

Highlight the most meaningful things you have written.

According to your life story check the following:

→ Are your goals aligned with your values?

→ What personal values do you need to practice daily?

→ Is this what you really want?

→ Are you worried about reaching others'
expectations?

→ Have you already accomplished some
things?

→ Are you on the right track?

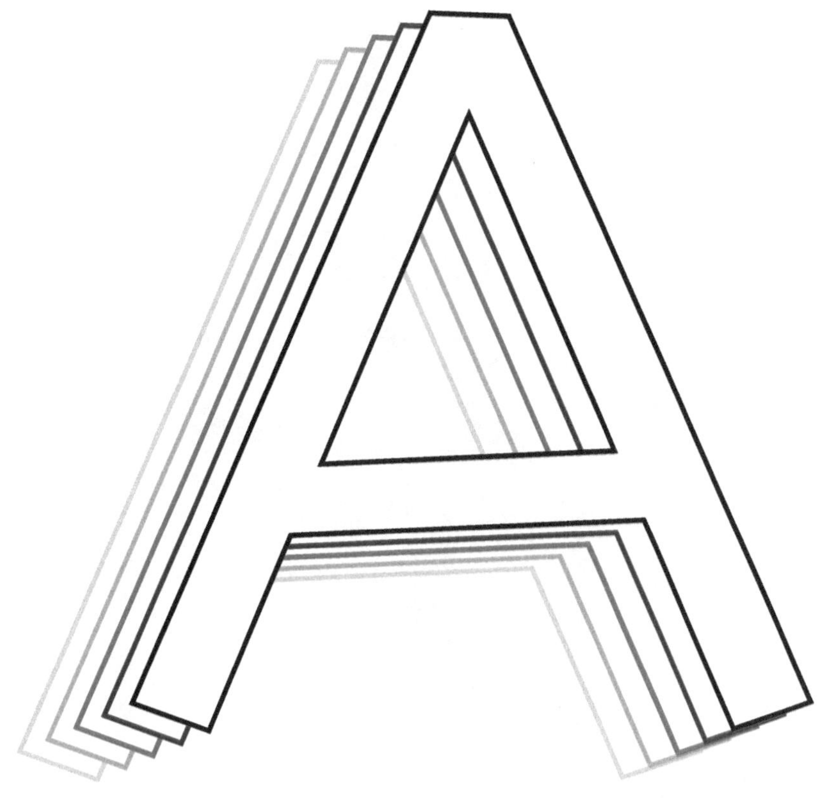

for Attitude

Your attitude is either the lock on or key to your door of success.

Denis Waitley

Let's define

Attitude

1 A position assumed for a specific purpose.

2 A settled way of thinking or feeling about someone or something, typically one that is reflected in a person's behavior.

3 A position of the body proper to or implying an action or mental state.

ATTITUDE

ATTITUDE

ATTITUDE

ATTITUDE

Now repeat out loud

NOW WORK IT,

OH YEAH!

WORK IT

Thru a positive mindset and healthy habits.

Learn to:

- Value
- Enjoy
- Rest
- Think
- Meditate
- Play and create
- Embrace the present moment

Do	Don't
Talk positive about yourself and others	Rumor, say or think badly about yourself and others
Look for inspiration: leaders, friends, family	Stick to toxic relationships or people who drain your energy
Focus on your talents and being authentic	Compare
Stay active	Stand still
Evaluate yourself: improvements you have made, goal-check, etc.	Overthink

Having a clear mind allows you to think and act with purpose. But, how?

Engage your five senses with things that improve your mood, stress levels and overall well being. For example, eating healthy boosts your energy, as it does surrounding yourself with positive people and investing your time in activities you enjoy.

If you like routines establish a **personal ritual** at the start and at the end of the day. Rituals assist you in renewing body, mind, and spirit in order to achieve your fullest potential.

Ideas:

- Take a shower.

- Listen to inspiring music that fills your senses and make you feel better.

- Drink coffee or tea in a beautiful mug.

- Meditate.

- Leave distractions as phones, news, tv, radio, tablets, etc.

- Call a friend or family to catch up.

- Take a walk

- Admire art: flowers, paintings, sculptures, nature.

❶ I will include in my morning routine:

❷ I will include in my evening routine:

Recognizing your emotions

- Be aware of **how** you are feeling and **why.**

- Recognize that sometimes it is ok not to be ok.

- According to Newton's third law of motion, every action has an equal and opposite reaction. Managing emotional reactions means choosing how and when to express the emotions we feel.

- Attitude does not mean being cheerful all the time and at our best, but to embrace "change as the only constant in life" as Heraclitus, a greek philosopher stated.

- To accept change means to identify obstacles and problems as a way of growing.

Our energies
must embrace

Problem » Acceptation » Change » Adaptation » Growth

This is what I call the
Growth Path

And change is continuous...

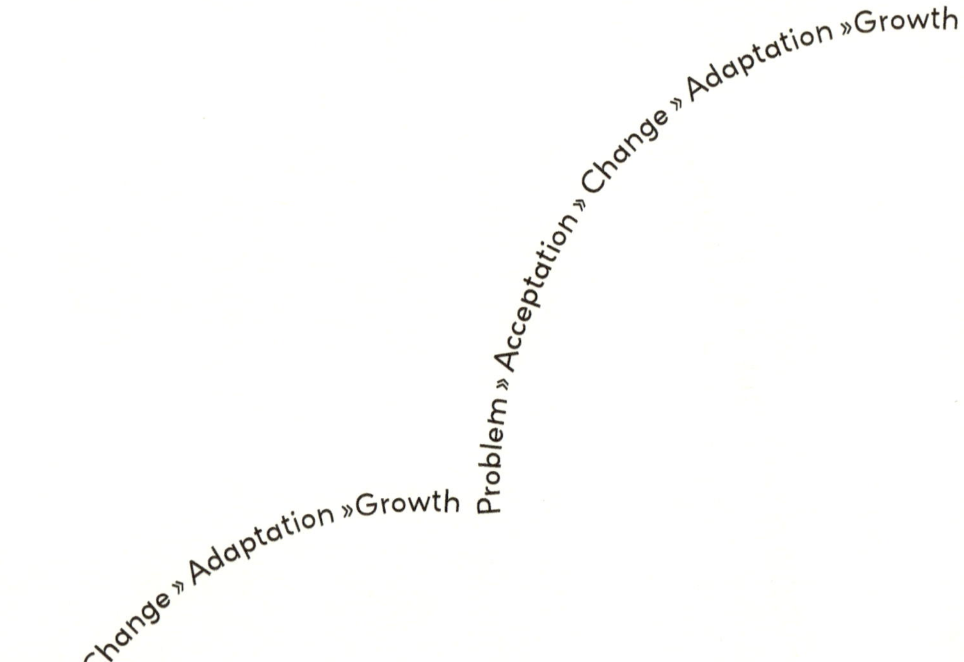

Problem » Acceptation » Change » Adaptation »Growth

Each obstacle or problem will make us stronger

Keep going, learning, failing and growing

To improve is to change; to be perfect is to change often.

Winston Churchill

Three basic questions that can raise awareness about our attitude toward one specific situation:

1. It depends on me? Go ahead and make it work!
2. It depends on **others**? You should not care, you can't do much to change it.
3. It depends on **the environment, destiny and time?** You can't do nothing either, so stop worrying about things you can not change.

Other questions you can ask yourself when worried...

- What's the issue?

- Why is it important?

- Will it matter tomorrow?

- Will it matter in a month?

- And in a year?

Maybe, is not such a BIG Deal as your mind pretends it to be.

GO FOR IT

1. Think of a good day, everything went right and you accomplished your goal or felt proud about yourself. How was your attitude?

2. Think of a bad day and describe your attitude.

3. Write down three things that make you feel better:

4. Write down three things you are thankful for:

5. Describe your attitude when:

• You are busy and someone demands your attention.

• You are on vacation.

• You are hungry.

• You had a good night's sleep.

• You feel unwell.

- Someone asks for your help.

- You ask someone for help.

- You learn something new.

- You did not get enough sleep.

- You win a prize.

- You lose a game.

- You have to wait for someone for a long time.

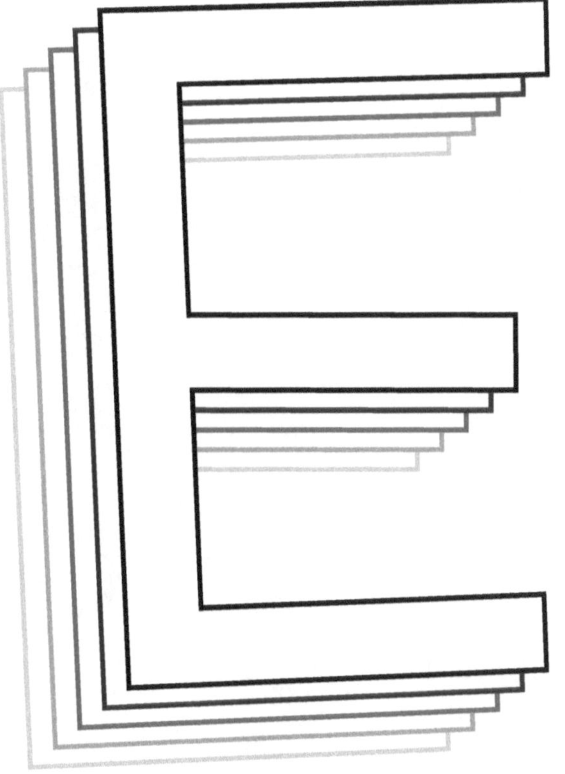

for **Effort**

If you want to be successful, find out what the price is and then pay it.

Scott Adam

Let's define

Effort

1 Physical or mental activity needed to achieve something.

2 A serious attempt to do something.

3 Exercise of physical or mental power.

Work hard play hard

Let's read this story...

Once upon a time there was a foodie king. He wanted to find the best food in the world.

He tried out all the food delivery services available in the market, asked his personal chef to choose the best ingredients and to experiment with all the cooking methods to find the best dish.

He was tired of eating too much of this and that. Ingredients from far away lands and homegrown were used to fulfill the king's desires. He explored all the cooking methods available: from fire and coal to microwave, oh, oh!

He asked his servants to gather the most delicious ingredients in the world. And they went off and bought a bit of everything. Sometimes it took weeks for his servants to find something new that would please the king's desire.

The day came when the servants were desperate because the king was running out of patience. His chancelor proposed to ask a wise man for advice. The wise man told the king he knew where to find what he was looking for: They would find it at the very top of the hill.

The king decided to go out on a quest with the wise man, who carried a bag full of things the king was unaware of.

Up and up they climbed. The first steps where easy, but as they walked and sometimes almost fell due to the harsh terrain, the king started complaining. The wise man never looked back because he was focused on getting all the way up to the top of the hill.

When they reached the top the king asked for the best food as was promised to him.

The wise man pulled out of his bag a piece of dry bread and a bottle of water and the king ate it as if it was the best thing he had ever tried.

The king understood that a person can appreciate more what is achieved through hard work.

That is the recipe.

From that day on, there was no need for his servants to look for the best ingredients or the best dish in the world. There were other issues that were solved.

WORK IT

Establish a big goal and milestones.

Learn to:

→ Motivate yourself

→ Plan your schedule

→ Rank your goals

→ Sacrifice for bigger gains in the future

→ Keep your goal in mind

→ Share your aspirations with people who can encourage, motivate and inspire you

→ Be aware that all great things require a significant amount of effort, sacrifice, intelligence and a supportive team

Do	**Don't**
Look for inspiration	Compare
Schedule self-care activities to regain strength	Burnout
Your goals must be timetable	Procrastinate
Be conscious some sacrifices are worth it: choose your battles wisely	Sacrifice your health and relationships for material wealth
Check your goals periodically and adjust to your needs and reality	Stick to goals that are no longer useful

- If you read or listen about leaders that changed the world most of them will agree their path was not easy. But all of them had a goal in mind and motivate themselves daily.

- Finding balance is personal and a never ending job. It requires self-awareness and openness to change.

- Let go of things and focus on what matters most to you. This won't be done once, but in a regular basis.

- Don't believe success comes by doing nothing.

Remember:

There's no such thing as a free lunch

Maslow's hierarchy of needs

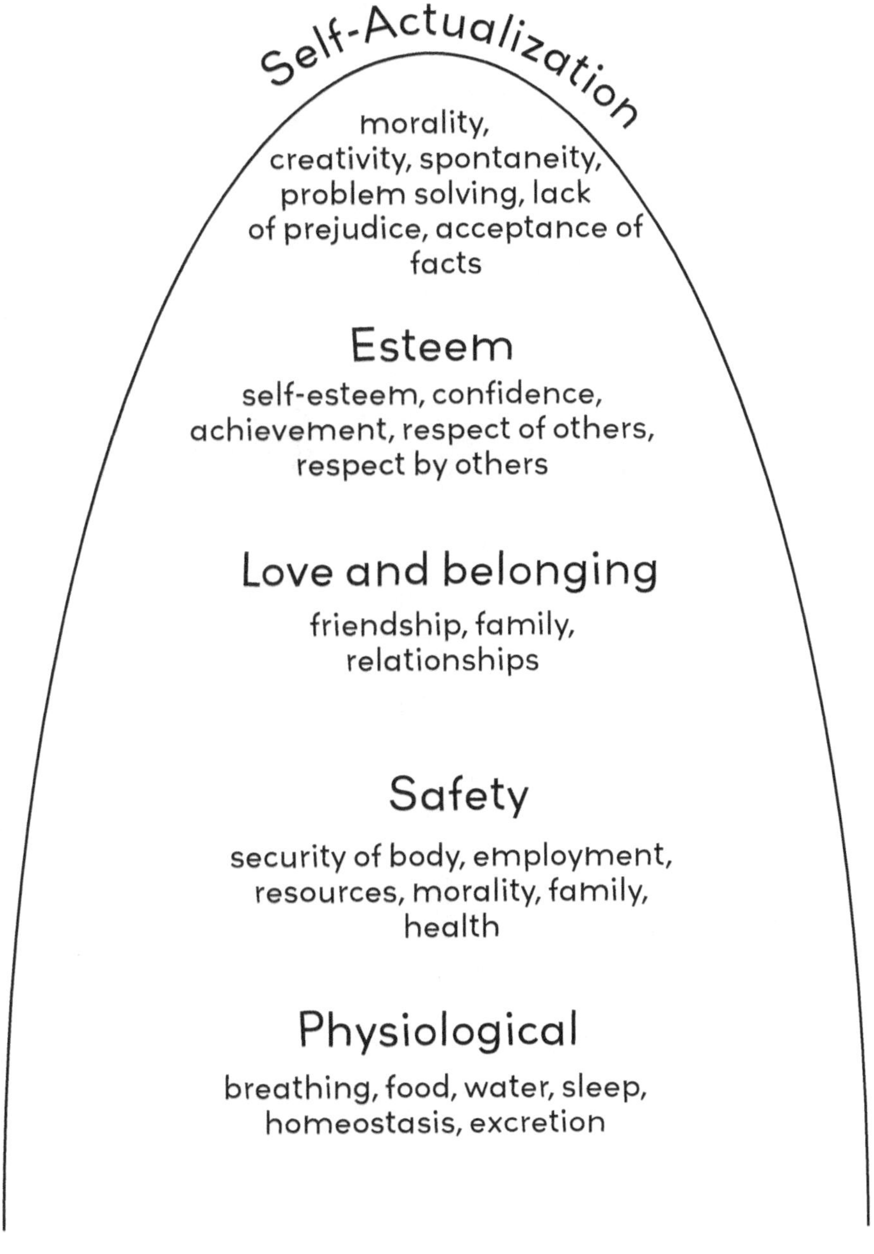

Remember

Life balance is personal

We are all different

We all have talents

I AM WORTHY

•

I CAN DO IT

•

I DESERVE LOVE AND BELONGING

Dream Big

- Write down your big goal:

- Write down your milestones:

- Draw your milestones and big goal.

- **What are you willing to sacrifice to achieve your goals?**

- **What are you not willing to sacrifice?**

GO FOR IT

Take action! What do you need to accomplish your big goal?

Personally:

1.
2.
3.
4.
5.

Financially:

1.
2.
3.
4.
5.

Other actions that need your attention:

1.
2.
3.
4.
5.

List some actions that are important for you and
your well-being in each stage of the pyramid.

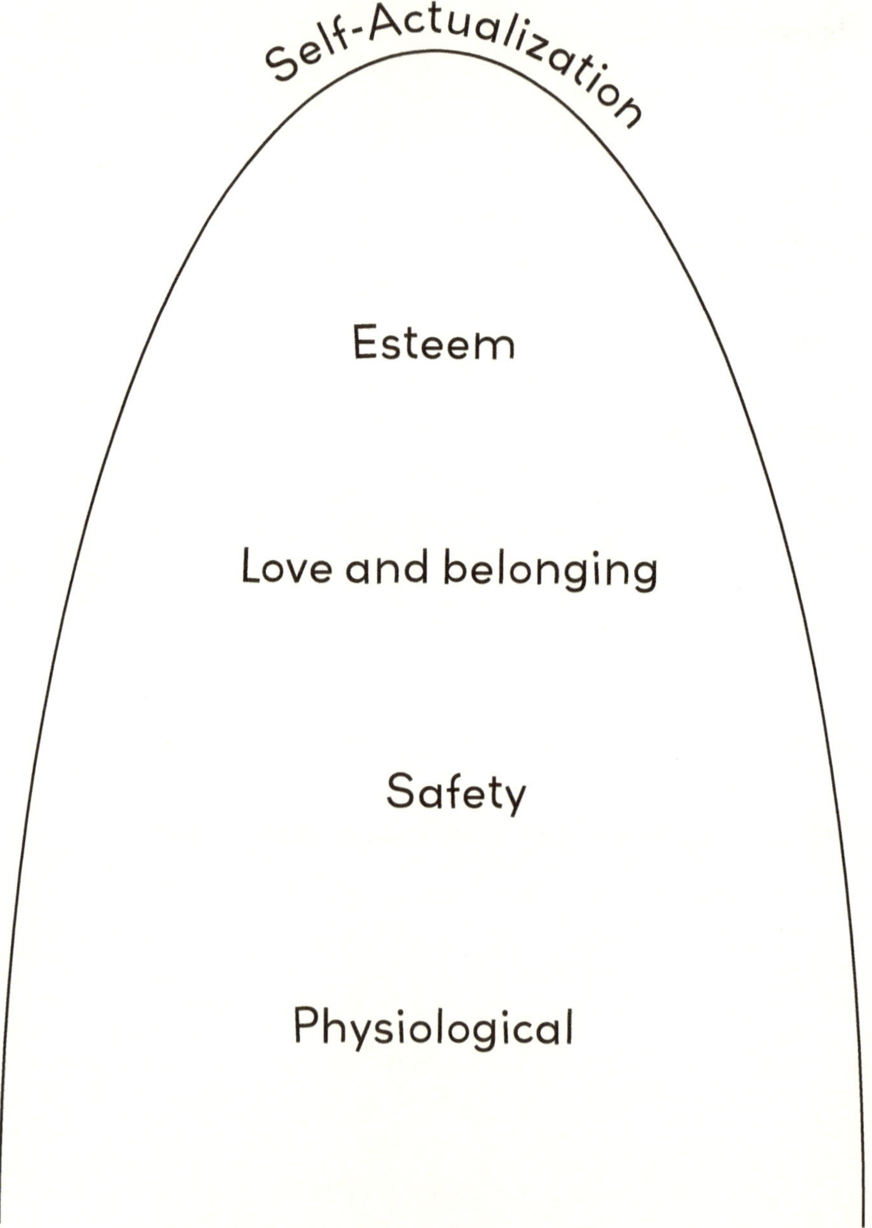

Only when we are brave enough
to explore the darkness
will we discover the infinite
power of our light.

Brené Brown

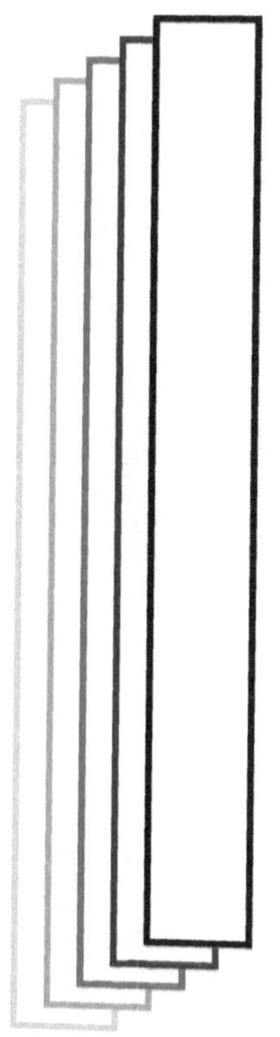

for Inspiration

If you are working on something that you really care about, you don't have to be pushed. The vision pulls you.

Steve Jobs

Let's define

Inspiration

1 The process of being mentally stimulated to do or feel something, especially to do something creative.

2 A sudden insight or leap in understanding that produces new, creative ideas or approaches to a problem.

3 Motivation, in which the individual strives to transmit, express, or actualize a new idea or vision.

GO AHEAD
THIS WAY
Wrong way
UP
DOWN

CHOOSE YOUR WAY

And to do so, you must answer:

What inspires you?

Such a simple question, so hard to answer.

When you think about inspiration, famous personalities, hardships and even certain moments in history might come to your mind. But, do they inspire you or affect you in an intense way?

Do they connect with you?

What drives you to take action?

The Tipping point

The book titled *The Tipping point: How Little Things Can Make a Big Difference* written by Malcolm Gladwell explains that the tipping point is that magic moment when an idea, trend or social behavior crosses a threshold, tips and spreads like wildfire.

When trying to identify the reason of "why" like why a song became popular, the reason why a company, product or brand became so known and wanted or how a video went viral, there's no logical explanation but that success occurs when **opportunity meets preparation.**

I once did a research to explain why some people decided to start their own business and start themselves as entrepreneurs and found out that all of them had a **tipping point.** One of them told me it was when the principal of his school asked him to get the highest grade on the national exam conducted by the government when he discovered he was capable of reaching outstanding academic results. Another entrepreneur told me it was because of his mother that pushed him hard and since he was a kid taught him to sell and make business.

Reasons may vary, but we all have **determining moments to discover our talents and make a difference.**

Each person that has reached a goal owns its story.

It might be someone familiar or not that can inspire us, a book, a video, a conference, a conversation... this book?

GET INSPIRED

Make a list of five personalities that inspire you and explain why.

Person	Actions and traits that inspire me

- Describe a moment when you felt inspired.

- Describe a historic event that inspires you.

Daily mood

- What inspired you to wake up this morning?

- How do you feel at the end of the day?

You have reached the pinnacle of success as soon as you become uninterested in money, compliments, or publicity.

Thomas Wolfe

When you find "that" thing that makes you wake up every morning no matter what, then you have found your source of inspiration.

It will come within.

Is an internal change one must embrace.

It does not come from money, others' behavior, fame or recognition.

Exercise to seek inspiration

1. Go to an open space or look out of a window.

2. Look at the sky and breath deeply.

3. Close your eyes.

4. Inhale and exhale 10 times, each time slower.

5. Put your hands together on a thank you pose over your heart.

6. Be aware of your breath and when you are in peace be grateful for what you have.

7. Breath deeply once again and open your eyes.

8. How do you feel?

Books that can help you inspire:

→ *The gifts of imperfection,* Brené Brown

→ *Atomic habits,* James Clear

→ *Start with why,* Simon Sinek

→ *Outliers,* Malcolm Gladwell

→ *The little book of Lykke,* Meik Wiking

→ *Permission to feel,* Marc Brackett

→ *The Subtle Art of Not Giving a F*ck,* Mark Manson

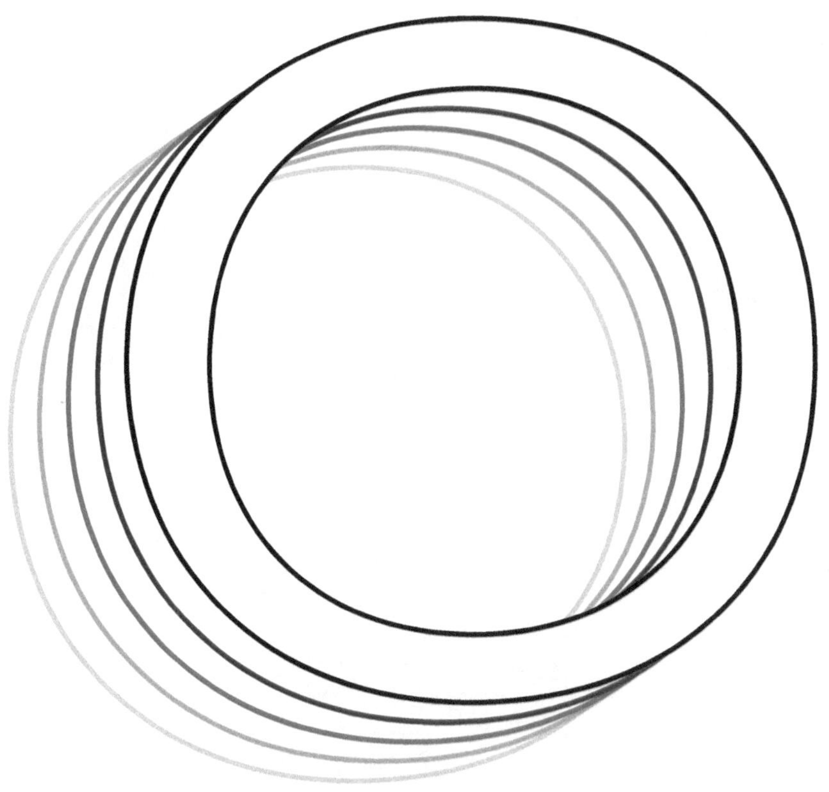

for Organization

Before anything else, **preparation** is the key to success.

Alexander Graham Bell

Let's define

ORGANIZATION

1 The planning of an activity or event.

2 The way in which something is done or arranged.

3 An efficient and orderly approach to tasks.

Self discipline means doing what you should rather than what you want to do

This quote goes against the well known belief of "you are free to do what you want to do". Well you literally are.

Yes.

But, if you want to achieve great things, they won't come alone.

Work hard Work smart

The road to success won't always be easy and it requires **discipline** and **hard work.** Some days will be better than others, but if we are able to discover what must be learnt in each stage of life and the steps toward achieving the big goal, the sacrifices will be worth it.

WORK SMART

Requires:

→ SELF-AWARENESS

→ SELF-EVALUATION

→ FLEXIBILITY

→ INNOVATION

ORGANIZATION MEANS PRIORIZATION

Prioritization is the art of combining everything we think we know about the past with the fixed resources we have right now to predict the order to do things to improve our collective future.

Let's define

Priority

A thing that is regarded as more important than another.

Let's talk about priorities

❶ Priorities are not standard.

There are things some people are able to trade off and others don't. Some value more good food, others prefer leisure activities. Some would prefer doing sports and others learning a new skill.

Each one of us is different.

❷ Priorities change.

They depend on:

- Age

- Stage of life

- Civil status

- Culture

- Physical and mental health

It is very likely that what matters most to you today is different than what did before, maybe a year or five years ago. It is very likely that your priorities in the future will be different as well.

We grow, we change and so do our priorities.

❸ Priorities must be meaningful.

Based on:

- Needs

- Strengths

- Values

- Goals

Think if it makes your life more meaningful.

EVERY DAY WE CHOOSE WHAT TO DO AND WHAT NOT TO DO.

This must be aligned with our path and big goal.

Tools to get organized and improve productivity

- Calendar/Agenda

- Timer

- Spreadsheets

- Smartphone reminders

- Keeping the workspace clean and organized

- Note-taking tool

- To-do list

Benefits:

- Save time

- Increase productivity

- Avoid mistakes

- Enable collaboration

- Aid memory

PRIORIZATION MATRIX

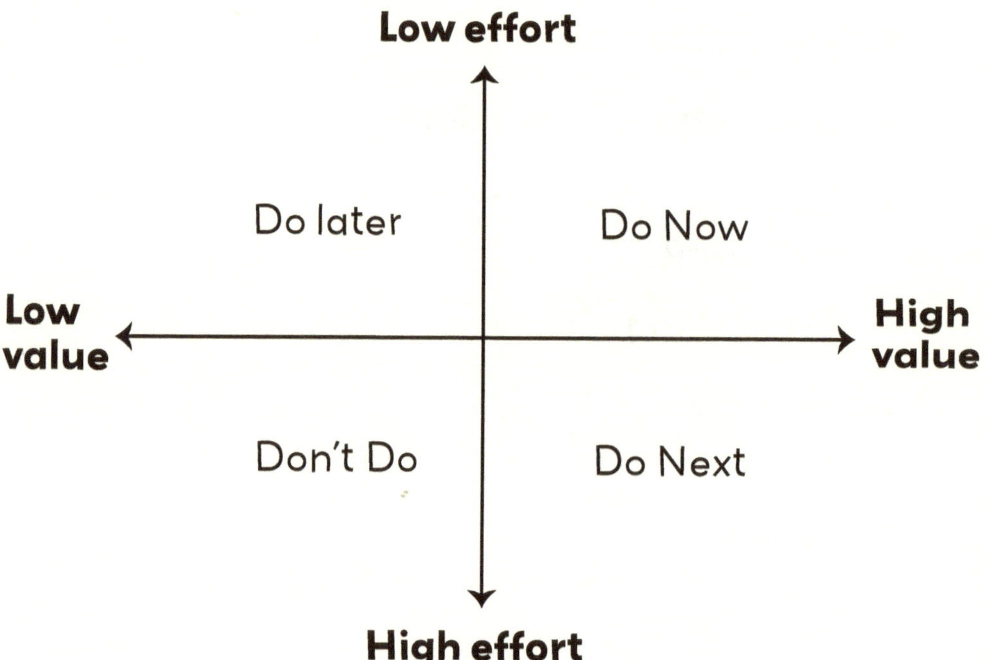

Think of activities you do all year round and write them down.

Complete the matrix with the activities you wrote according to its relevance.

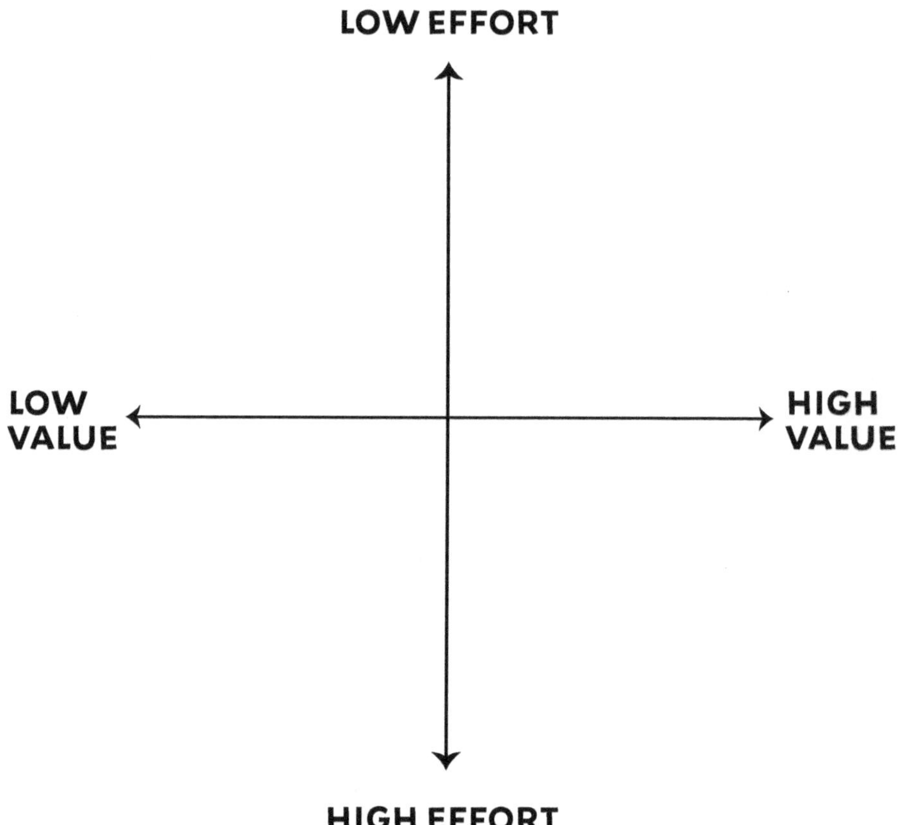

List daily activities.

Complete the matrix with the activities you wrote.

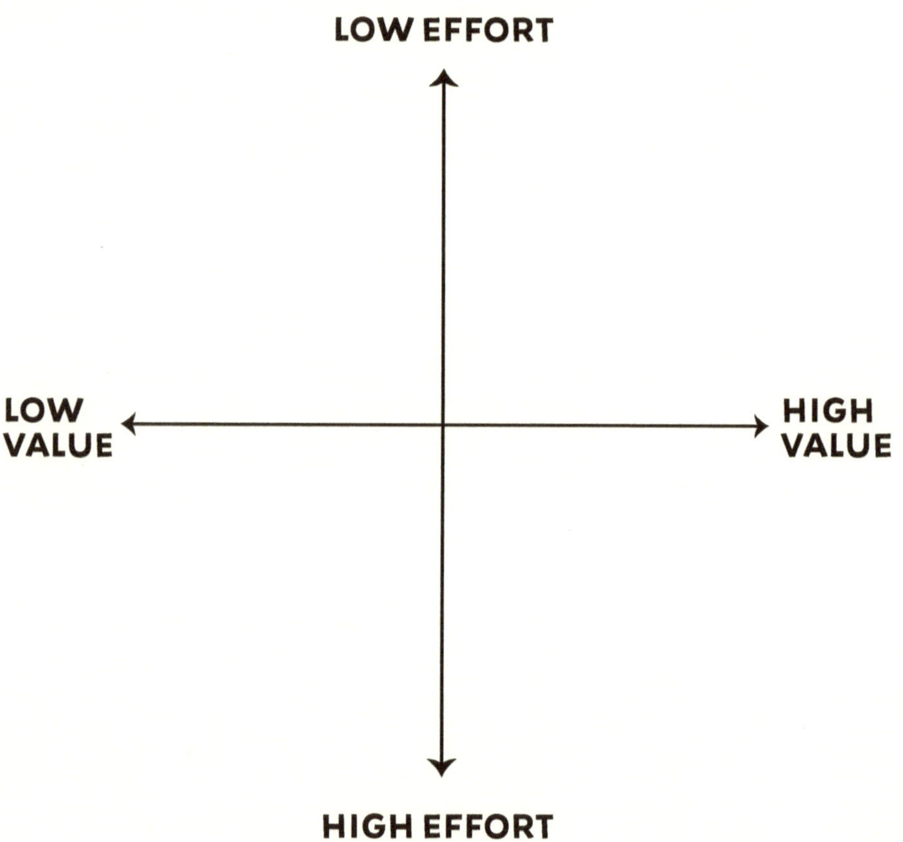

Think of how much time of your day you invest in each of the following tasks. Do you want to invest more or less time in each task? Color the symbol accordingly.

Action	Time spent each day
sleeping	✚ ▢
eating	✚ ▢
self-care	✚ ▢
meditation	✚ ▢
TV or series	✚ ▢
working	✚ ▢
studying	✚ ▢
social media	✚ ▢
reading	✚ ▢
other:	✚ ▢

Think of how much time of your day you want to invest in each of the following activities.

Action	Time spent each day
sleeping	
eating	
self-care	
meditation	
TV or series	
working	
studying	
social media	
reading	
other:	

A common day would look like this:

Time	Activity

Things I can change on my daily routine to have a more meaningful day:

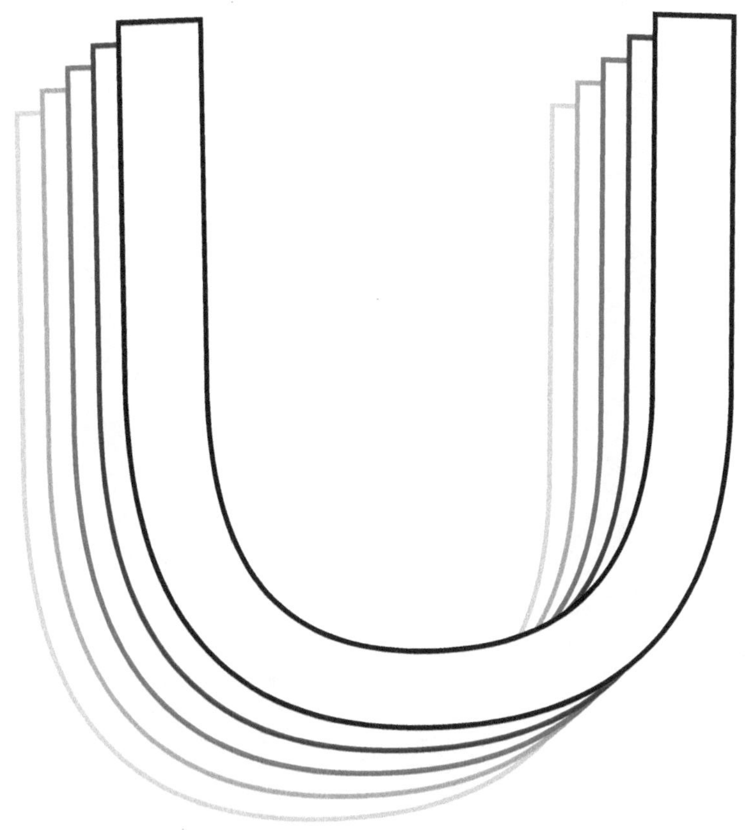

for You

It's about you

Being you.

Yes,

YOU

No one else but you.

Knowing yourself is the beginning of all wisdom.

Aristotle

Recognize your talents through self-awareness.

- How much do you know yourself?

- What do you want?

- What are your needs?

- What inspires you?

Love yourself first
and everything
else falls into line.
You really have to
love yourself to get
anything done in
this world.

Lucille Ball

All about you

1. How much do **you** know yourself? Highlight the option that suits you the best.

Wake up early	Stay up late
Coffee	Tea
City	Country
Read a book	Watch TV
Gym	Outdoor sport
Mountain	Beach
Big house	Small place
Ride a car	Walk or ride a bike
Text	Call
Sneakers	Sandals
Rice	Pasta
Meat	Salad
Sunny day	Rainy day
Hot	Cold
Quiet	Loud
Jeans	Shorts
Animals	Plants
Travel	Shopping
Family	Friends
Indoor	Outdoor
Monochromatic	Colorful
Winter	Summer
Autumn	Spring
Water	Other:

Neither option is better than the other. If you can compare your answers with a friend this can help you learn about each other's preferences.

2. Write down an emotion that you relate to each of the following actions.

- To hang out with a friend:

- To hang out with my family:

- Giving a gift:

- Receiving a gift:

- Giving a compliment:

- Receiving a compliment:

- Planning a trip:

- Cancelling a plan:

- Reschedule an important event:

- Being at work:

- Studying __________:

- Exercising:

- Being alone:

- Being with other people:

3. Read the following emotions: happy, sad, angry, scared. Think of a moment in your life you relate with each emotion.

sad	happy
angry	scared

4. Describe a moment you felt loved.

5. List 10 acts of love you have with the ones around you.

6. Name a place where you feel safe and describe how you feel when you are there.

7. Write the names of people you feel comfortable with.

8. Write down prejudices about yourself.

9. Rewrite them in a positive way.

10. What are you scared of?

11. Choose one of your fears and try to remember when and why it started. Can you do something about it?

12. Join the dots and find something that relates to you.

13.   Highlight with your favorite colors the first seven words you come up to.

youjuolaareaspecielsaaakolavelaughandgo
hojoloaheadahaulikoandsavealotofgood
energiesthroughthisandthatmiguebecauze
lifeisamazingandvictfilyoumustembrace
litotogratefulandfililiveforguveandtake
allofthatshotandmakeitvictorinacomeon
andworthitforgivewhetjojojajlaothankfulca
ryingworkmatterevenanrelationshiphealthy
jolajnbiucbuicicniocroicjricodnsahabits
aklogoodfeelingsundvibesajablessings
couragehplalahuxjcijcbuolovigolameant
tobeuyhbraveenoughhuakahsullifeasitis

14.   Write a personal motto using the words you highlighted.

____

____

15.   Who are you? Describe yourself as a loved
      and valuable being.

16.   Ask someone close to describe you and compare it with what you wrote.

17.   Write down how this made you feel.

GIVING THROUGH RECEIVING

Sometimes we are not willing to accept help or accept a gift. Why? Reasons may vary, but recognizing our value leads to valuing others as well.

- You can't give what you don't have.

- You can't share if you don't have something to offer.

- One must be full to spread.

A better me is coming...

If you found this book helpful
please share it and leave a review

THANK YOU